To

From

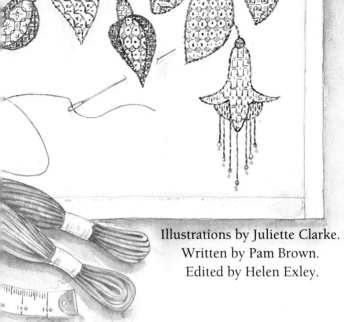

Illustrations by Juliette Clarke.
Written by Pam Brown.
Edited by Helen Exley.

Other mini books in the Exley series
To a very Special Friend   To my very Special Love
To a Special Grandmother   To a Special Mother
To my very Special Husband   To my very Special Wife

Published in Great Britain in 1991 by Exley Publications Ltd
First published in the USA in 1992 by Exley Giftbooks
Illustrations copyright © Exley Publications 1991
Selection copyright © Helen Exley 1991
Reprinted November 1991
Third, fourth, fifth and sixth printings 1992
ISBN 1-85015-278-0
A copy of the CIP data is available from the British Library on request.
Designed by Pinpoint Design Company.
Printed and bound in Hungary.
Exley Publications Ltd., 16 Chalk Hill, Watford, Herts WD1 4BN, United Kingdom.
Exley Giftbooks, 359 East Main Street, Suite 3D, Mount Kisco, NY 10549, USA.
*Dedication: To my own dear daughters, Helen and Sarah and my extra daughter, Eve, from Mum.
With love and thanks and three rousing cheers.*

I often wondered before you came how I would handle a daughter. Did I want a frilly daughter or a chunky, cheerful child? Did I want her to be an administrator? Or caring? Or both?

As it was, I didn't get any of my dreams. I got a totally unique, totally new, totally puzzling, unpredictable, delightful you.

. . .

I keep an album of photographs of you – as if I could hold on to all the different yous – the baby, the toddler, the school girl, the teenager. But they don't really matter. Not that much. Because you are all of them – and every time I see you I think, "*This* is the best time."

. . .

Dear daughter. I think of you *all* the time. When I
find the dye from your
T-shirt has patterned most things in the wash.
When I find long hairs in the drain pipe. When I'm
scrubbing the bath oil scum off the bath. When I
find a half-eaten bar of chocolate in your bed. When
I discover you've consumed *all* the ice-cream, just
before dinner. When I find a yoghurt-pot full of
primroses by my bed.
I love you.

. . .

Thanks for all the cards – hand drawn or by Renoir.
For all the parcels – knobbly or beribboned. For all
the hurried kisses – smelling of chocolate or Chanel.
For remembering.

. . .

Sometimes I wish I had the power to make things come right for you. Sometimes I wish I had money enough to give you the things you dream of. Sometimes I wish I had treasures to pass on to you. But I gave what I could – your five bright senses, the world about you. Take what you want, add your own wonder to the sum of all human wonder, and pass on the gift of love.

It is enough.

. . .

Dear daughter. I wish you eyes to see – the gull's gawkish walk, the turn of leaves, the coil of running water, the spurt of raindrops on a shining street, ▷

rainbows, a swirl of starlings in a city sky.

I wish you ears to hear – the murmur of hidden streams, a morning robin, scufflings in the hedgerow, the sound of traffic muted by summer trees, anchor cable running out, the hush of voices as the curtain rises.

Smells haunting and sharp, enticing, evanescent. The first violets, clean linen, roast chestnuts.

The touch of silk and sun-warmed stone. Cats. And familiar, loving hands.

The taste of new bread, of clear water, of the *vin du pays*, of a newly-picked tomato.

Dear daughter – I wish you life.

Daughters are given to making announcements. I'm joining an ashram. I've signed on to crew a boat to Singapore. I've invited my headteacher to dinner. . . Today. I'm getting a tattoo. I'm leaving home. I'm going to be a nun. I'm in love with an Arab sheik. I'm moving back home. I'm having my hair dyed pink. I'm going to settle down just as soon as I've sailed around the Horn.

Having daughters is the best investment you will ever make against becoming bored.

. . .

Life since you came has been like an extraordinary book – one where I just can't wait to turn the page and see what new thing you have done. I don't know which I like best – the quiet chapters – or the big dramatic scenes – or the cliff-hangers. It's never dull.I just can't get over the fact that I had a hand in the authorship.

. . .

IN PRAISE

I'm proud of all your achievements. You've worked hard for them. I'm proud of your looks and your intelligence – which some far distant ancestor handed down. But I'm most proud of your being just *you*. 'Success' would be an extra – but you are special to me *whatever* you do.

. . .

I'm proud of you not for the things that came easily to you – or that were part of you from the very beginning – but for your slogging it out against the odds and against your nature and spluttering to the surface with your prize.

. . .

No. You are not perfect – and I am sorry that when you were small I sometimes seemed to demand perfection. You are better than perfect. You are a unique piece of humanity, fallible, questing, always astonishing in your discoveries and dreams. I am everlastingly thankful that a little of me is caught up in your being, and that you carry me into a future that I shall never know.

You are all of us – and yet yourself forever.

. . .

In a world where it is necessary to succeed, perhaps only we women know more deeply that success can be a quiet and hidden thing.

. . .

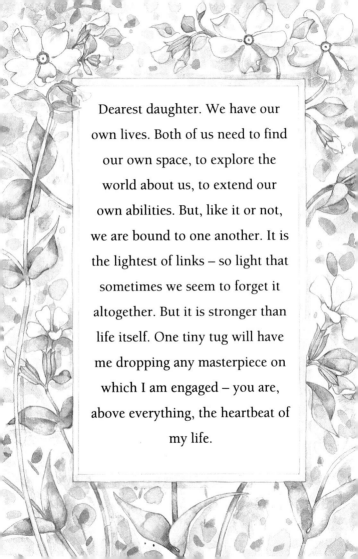

Dearest daughter. We have our own lives. Both of us need to find our own space, to explore the world about us, to extend our own abilities. But, like it or not, we are bound to one another. It is the lightest of links – so light that sometimes we seem to forget it altogether. But it is stronger than life itself. One tiny tug will have me dropping any masterpiece on which I am engaged – you are, above everything, the heartbeat of my life.

We've done well – seen wonders, dreamed dreams. Perhaps we haven't made a circumnavigation of the world, or climbed Everest, or written a best seller.

Yet.

We've different tastes, different skills, different ambitions. But we like to watch the other live and learn – and to applaud when it's called for. Perhaps we're not everyone's conventional idea of a mother and daughter. Perhaps there's no such thing.

But we like each other. We encourage each other. We are friends.

. . .

When I am feeling weary
and all the world is dreary
with thin incessant rain,
I think about my daughter,
her brightness and her laughter,
and life comes right again.

. . .

Never forget – you're not just special
to me. You're special. And that's
that.

. . .

I *could* say you were the cleverest,
the most beautiful, the most
perceptive, even-tempered, wise,
considerate daughter in the *entire*
universe. But that wouldn't be right.
I've not *met* all the daughters in the
universe. I can only judge by my
limited acquaintance.
But on *that* basis I say you are the
cleverest, the most beautiful, the
most. . . .

. . .

<u>THANK YOU!</u>

Thank you for having given me the chance to make mud pies again, to paddle in the sea, to sail toy boats, to ride the fairground horses, to try everything in the children's museum exhibit – and to stroke all the goats in the children's zoo. Thank you for an excuse to make home-made jam and bake birthday cakes. Thank you for bringing back fun to all our lives.

. . .

Thank you for believing my birthday cakes were magical, my paintings amazing and my stories were the best in the world.

Sometimes when I'm feeling particularly useless you give me sound advice – which I once gave you. It cheers me up no end. Thanks for keeping an eye on me, love.

. . .

It is always a surprise to find you have a daughter as young as yourself.

Thank you, dear, for not thinking I am old.

Or, at least, not *that* old.

. . .

The best thing you have given me is your friendship.

. . .

YOUR GIFTS TO ME

A child gives us our own first times all over
again. I have watched the marvel of a curtain
– rise in your face, the hushing of a concert
hall as the baton lifts, the first sight of the sea.
Thank you for reawakening wonder.

. . .

Thank you for wilting dandelions,
for twigs of lambstails, for wet pebbles,
for fluff-covered toffees, for sticky kisses.
Thank you for loving me.
Some daughters give florist's bouquets,
Cartier watches and *Cointreau*. Some
daughters send shrubs, sweaters and
home-made jam. The thing is – daughters
know *exactly* what one needs.

Thank you, my dearest girl, for telling me
when your friend is in trouble, even though
there's nothing I can do to be of any help.

Thank you for newspaper articles you
thought might interest me.

Thank you for the phone call to tell me of a
TV documentary that's just starting.

Thank you for birthday cards that are
exactly right.

Thank you for asking me for recipes.

Thank you for giving me advice.

Thank you for letting me into your life.

. . .

Thank you for showing me, when I thought
my mothering days were over, that the best
days between us are only just beginning.

April 5.
S.W.A.L.K.
my love &
M. Barbosa,
Lower Farm,
Nalton St,
May 21
You are invited to.....
t me for lunch 12 o'clock
Sat 26th
be a

There is nothing, absolutely nothing
that can cheer up a dismal evening of
TV repeats and yesterday's leftovers
more successfully than a phone call
from a daughter.

. . .

With you away adventuring, the house seems very
flubsy and dull. My mind half makes plans to go to
sea again, or cross the Sahara in a Land Rover or
some such. But then I catch sight of myself in the
mirror and I realize sadly that my shinning-up-the-
rigging and brewing-up-in-camp days are over.
You'll just have to do it for me. Have as much fun
and excitement as I did. Boil the water. Shake the
bedding. Keep your feet in good order.
And write your diary.
My mind and heart are with you.

. . .

You will choose your own faith. Perhaps you will revere a god, a prophet, a teacher. All I ask is that you show reverence for every living thing that shares your world. If you must destroy, destroy only from necessity and with full knowledge of what you do. We are indissolubly linked one with the other.

. . .

You have to fight your own battles, love. But I'm here in your corner with the bucket and sponge.

. . .

When you were very small I could kiss most things better. Or soothe it with a spoonful of gripewater. I could mend most things that a kiss couldn't cure – with glue and tape, a needle and thread, elastic, staples, string. I was very good at replacing dolls' eyeballs – and arms and legs. And hair. But now there are things I cannot stick together, or heal with a hug. Grown up matters beyond my skills. I wish I had some magic that could make such things come right. All I can do is be here. Always.

. . .

HOPES AND DREAMS

My hope for you is that all your life you will go on being astonished and delighted by the world about you.

. . .

Of course I dream I could give you all the places I couldn't take you – Florence and Venice and Rome, Paris and Prague, the Isles of Greece, Leningrad. But you might not want them. I wish you your own places, your own adventures, your own loves.

. . .

No, love, I don't dream of wealth and success for you. Only a job you like, skills you can perfect, enthusiasms to lighten your heart, friends and love in abundance.

. . .

Dearest – with all these technical wonders around us I'm going to wish you something incredibly old fashioned. The joy of reading books. Books unmolested by Hollywood, Theme Parks, Digests or Strip Cartoonists. Just books. One mind speaking to another across time and space.

. . .

Dear. I hope that when you are very, *very* old you can look back and say "Heavens. That was a *lovely* life."

. . .

You have my love – the love that links us. Take it with you into the world that I will never know.

. . .

MY WISHES FOR YOU

I wish you happy and secure and comfortable and wise. But not yet. Get the adventures in first.

. . .

I wish you the passion that creates and pray the passion that destroys passes you by.

. . .

How can I wish you anything? Save that you find what you want to do and do it. Well.

. . .

I wish you the beauty of silence, the glory of sunlight, the mystery of darkness, the force of flame, the power of water, the sweetness of air, the quiet strength of earth, the love that lies at the very root of things. I wish you the wonder of living.

What do I *most* wish for you?

A belief in the fundamental worth of human kind,
and that, my dear, includes yourself.

. . .

I wish you love. Romance, yes. But, too, the love of
those who lie together in the darkness, talking of
times past. The reaching up of children's arms, the
honey-sticky kisses. The butt of a small cat's head. A
dog's companionable sigh. The reassuring touch, the
lighting up of eyes, the sound of a key in the lock.

. . .

I wish you a daughter just like you.

. . .